Student Workbook

AGS PUBLISHING

Life Skills English

by
Bonnie L. Walker

AGS Publishing
Circle Pines, Minnesota 55014-1796
1-800-328-2560

Printed in the United States of America

ISBN 0-7854-3067-9
Product Number 93623

A 0 9 8 7 6 5 4 3 2

Table of Contents

Workbook Activity   1   Alphabetical Order

Workbook Activity   2   Alphabetical Lists

Workbook Activity   3   Using Guide Words

Workbook Activity   4   Using Guide Words

Workbook Activity   5   Knowing What to Look Up

Workbook Activity   6   Looking Up Related Subjects

Workbook Activity   7   Where to Look for Information

Workbook Activity   8   Using the Internet

Workbook Activity   9   Understanding Dictionary Entries

Workbook Activity   10   More About Dictionary Entries

Workbook Activity   11   Using Dictionary Entries

Workbook Activity   12   Using Dictionaries to Check Spelling

Workbook Activity   13   Using Dictionaries to Find Facts

Workbook Activity   14   Almanacs

Workbook Activity   15   Atlases

Workbook Activity   16   Maps

Workbook Activity   17   Encyclopedias

Workbook Activity   18   Cookbooks

Workbook Activity   19   Food Labels

Workbook Activity   20   How-to Books

Workbook Activity   21   Magazines

Workbook Activity   22   Magazine Facts

Workbook Activity   23   Telephone Books

Workbook Activity   24   Using Telephone Books

Workbook Activity   25   Telephone Numbers

Workbook Activity   26   Telephone Service Providers and Bills

Workbook Activity   27   Cell Phones and Phone Cards

Workbook Activity   28   What's in a Library?

Workbook Activity   29   Fiction Books

Workbook Activity   30   The Dewey Decimal System

Workbook Activity 31   Using the Dewey Decimal System

Workbook Activity 32   Periodicals and Audiovisuals

Workbook Activity 33   Finding Information in a Library

Workbook Activity 34   Television

Workbook Activity 35   Radio

Workbook Activity 36   Newspapers

Workbook Activity 37   Advertisements

Workbook Activity 38   Classified Ads

Workbook Activity 39   Help-Wanted Ads

Workbook Activity 40   Reading Help-Wanted Ads

Workbook Activity 41   Professionals

Workbook Activity 42   Help from Other Experts

Workbook Activity 43   Occupational Titles

Workbook Activity 44   Organizations

Workbook Activity 45   Getting Help from Organizations

Workbook Activity 46   Personal Information

Workbook Activity 47   Job Application Forms

Workbook Activity 48   Filling Out Job Application Forms

Workbook Activity 49   Job Application Acrostic

Workbook Activity 50   Previous Work Experience

Workbook Activity 51   Employment History

Workbook Activity 52   Financial Forms

Workbook Activity 53   Establishing Credit

Workbook Activity 54   Reading Catalogs

Workbook Activity 55   Internet Shopping

Workbook Activity 56   Ordering Products

Workbook Activity 57   Ordering from a Catalog

Workbook Activity 58   Filling Out an Order Form

Workbook Activity 59   Returning Products

Workbook Activity 60   Addressing an Envelope

Alphabetical Order

Directions Rewrite each list in alphabetical order.

HINT Ignore hyphens and apostrophes when you alphabetize.
TIP Look up the words in your dictionary you do not know.

EXAMPLE

1. whereas __wharf__
2. wheat __what__
3. when __whatever__
4. whatsoever __whatnot__
5. wheelchair __whatsoever__

6. whatever __wheat__
7. wheel __wheel__
8. wharf __wheelchair__
9. whatnot __when__
10. what __whereas__

List A:

1. canon _____
2. can't _____
3. can _____
4. canning _____
5. canvas _____

6. cannon _____
7. canyon _____
8. candle _____
9. candlestick _____
10. canned _____

List B:

1. do-it-yourself _____
2. dodge _____
3. do _____
4. done _____
5. don't _____

6. does _____
7. doe _____
8. door _____
9. donkey _____
10. dome _____

Alphabetical Lists

Directions Rewrite each list in alphabetical order.

EXAMPLE

Common Last Names

1. Howard ___Hamelton___
2. Harrison ___Hamilton___
3. Hewitt ___Hammel___
4. Henry ___Harding___
5. Hammel ___Hardy___
6. Hamelton ___Harris___
7. Hamilton ___Harrison___
8. Harding ___Henry___
9. Harris ___Hewitt___
10. Hardy ___Howard___

List A: Budget Items

1. groceries _____
2. rent _____
3. utilities _____
4. taxes _____
5. clothing _____
6. furniture _____
7. insurance _____
8. gasoline _____
9. entertainment _____
10. savings _____

List B: Baseball Hall of Famers
Alphabetize these names last name first.

1. Home Run Baker _____
2. Sandy Koufax _____
3. Early Wynn _____
4. Satchel Paige _____
5. Stan Musial _____

Name _____ Date _____ Period _____

Using Guide Words

Directions Read each set of guide words and the four words under each set. Circle the words you would find on a page with the guide words.

EXAMPLE   hockey .... holly
   A home   **C** hobby
   B hoe   **D** hole

1. grade .... grandmother
   A grate   **C** graduate
   B graph   **D** grain

2. dollar .... dooryard
   A dock   **C** donkey
   B dolphin   **D** doormat

3. script .... scurry
   A seaport   **C** search
   B scythe   **D** scrub

4. giant .... girl scout
   A ginger   **C** germ
   B giggle   **D** ghost

5. match .... mattress
   A mate   **C** may
   B mat   **D** math

6. well-grounded .... we've
   A well-informed **C** western
   B well-read   **D** we're

7. afternoon .... agree
   A after   **C** agreeable
   B age   **D** agency

8. busboy .... butterfat
   A burden   **C** but
   B butter   **D** busy

9. friendship .... frozen
   A fruit   **C** front
   B frosting   **D** frown

10. newsworthy .... night
   A newspaper   **C** nickname
   B NH   **D** niece

Using Guide Words

Directions For each group of words below, provide two guide words that could be found at the top of the dictionary page. You may use a dictionary for guide word ideas.

(EXAMPLE)   improvement, inch, include
Guide words: <u>*impress* and *increase*</u>

---

1. global, globe, gloom

    Guide words: _____

2. bed, bee, beeper

    Guide words: _____

3. before, begin, behave

    Guide words: _____

4. anger, answerable, ant

    Guide words: _____

5. knight, knock, knot

    Guide words: _____

6. jam, janitor, Japan

    Guide words: _____

7. forehand, forehead, forever

    Guide words: _____

8. tangle, tank, tape

    Guide words: _____

9. update, upper, upset

    Guide words: _____

10. moray eel, more, morning

    Guide words: _____

Knowing What to Look Up

The English language is very rich. Almost every person, place, thing, or idea has more than one name. A word that has the same or almost the same meaning as another word is called a *synonym*.

Directions Write a synonym for each of the following words. You may use a thesaurus.

(**EXAMPLE**) ask _question_____

1. yell _____

2. doctor _____

3. beautiful _____

4. town _____

5. stream _____

6. supper _____

7. woman _____

8. sofa _____

9. food _____

10. popular _____

11. tall _____

12. thin _____

13. swimming _____

14. dog _____

15. topic _____

Looking Up Related Subjects

If you are unable to find the exact word you are looking for in an index or library catalog, you need to think of a related subject.

Directions Here is a list of topics. Write a word or phrase that you could look up in a library catalog or index for each topic. You may use a dictionary for help.

(EXAMPLE) editing videotapes __video production, editing__
trombone __instruments, horns__

1. how to replace a car battery _____

2. raising Holsteins _____

3. geraniums _____

4. parachutes _____

5. lemonade _____

6. Jupiter _____

7. Neil Armstrong _____

8. Scotland _____

9. mink _____

10. country music _____

11. Appaloosa _____

12. watermelon _____

13. modems _____

14. bachelor of arts _____

15. spaghetti _____

Where to Look for Information

From the book *Programming for Fun and Profit*

Contents

1 Getting Started 5
2 Computer Languages 7
    BASIC 8
    Cobol 11
    Fortran 14
    Pascal 17
3 Business Applications 21
    Database management 23
    Spreadsheets 30
    Word processing 39
4 Selecting a Computer 51
    Price ranges 53
    Capabilities 54

Index

BASIC, 8, 21–23
Business applications 21–50
    (see also Using computers)
    database, 23
    spreadsheets, 30
    word processing, 39
Cobol, 11
Computers, 7, 53–60
    capabilities, 54
    languages, 7
    price ranges, 53
    selecting, 51–58
Database management, 23
Fortran, 14
Pascal, 17

Directions Study the samples above. Then answer the questions that follow.

EXAMPLE   Which pages have information about BASIC? **pages 8, 21–23** _____

1. On which page does the discussion about word processing begin? _____

2. On which page could you find information about Pascal? _____

3. What are BASIC, Cobol, Fortran, and Pascal? _____

4. What subject would you read about on page 23? _____

5. In which chapter can you learn about computer price ranges? _____

6. Which page has information about word processing? _____

7. Which page has information about spreadsheets? _____

8. Which chapter includes information about getting started? _____

9. Which pages help you select a computer? _____

10. What is the main difference between an index and a table of contents? _____

Using the Internet

Directions Write the key words you would type into an Internet search engine to find information on the following topics.

(**EXAMPLE**)   movies in which your favorite actor has starred __movies, the actor's name__

1. the planet closest to the Sun _____

2. directions to a city you have never visited _____

3. names for baby girls and baby boys _____

4. Internet auction sites _____

5. paying taxes online _____

6. prices for skateboard wheels _____

7. medical information on arthritis _____

8. public libraries in your town _____

9. information on jobs in your area _____

10. the telephone number for a local carpenter _____

11. information about ancient Egypt _____

12. caring for parakeets _____

13. recent earthquakes _____

14. Canadian wildlife _____

15. books written by F. Scott Fitzgerald _____

Understanding Dictionary Entries

Directions Study the entry. Then follow the directions.

> **sweet** (swēt) *adj.* [OE, akin to *swot*] **1**: having a taste of, or like that of, sugar
> **2 a**: having a generally agreeable taste, smell, sound, appearance: PLEASANT
> **b**: agreeable to the mind: GRATIFYING **c**: having a friendly, pleasing disposition
> **3 a**: not rancid, spoiled, sour, or fermented **b**: not salty or salted – **sweet** *n.*
> something sweet, as a sweet food – **sweet•ly** *adv.* – **sweet•ness** *n.* –
> **sweet•ish** *adj.*

EXAMPLE   Write the entry word. _sweet_____

1. Count the number of syllables in this word. Write the number. _____

2. Write the phonetic spelling of this word. Say the word aloud. _____

3. What is the part of speech of the first set of meanings of this word? _____

4. Count all of the meanings for *sweet* as an adjective. How many are given? _____

5. Write one synonym for *sweet*. _____

6. What does *sweet* mean when we use it as a noun? _____

7. Write another adjective form of *sweet*. _____

8. Write the adverb form of *sweet*. _____

9. Write another noun form of *sweet*. _____

10. For each sentence, identify the part of speech of each word in bold.

    _____   **A** The **sweetness** of the apple was pleasant.

    _____   **B** Joan smiled **sweetly** at her mother.

    _____   **C** The peaches had a **sweetish** taste.

    _____   **D** My! But, you are a **sweet** person.

    _____   **E** "**Sweets** to the sweet" is an old saying.

More About Dictionary Entries

Directions Use a dictionary to find the answers to these questions.

EXAMPLE What happens during a **stampede**?
A herd of animals rush by suddenly.

---

1. Was **Robin Hood** a real person?

_____

2. What is the first name of the **Rockefeller** who was vice president
of the United States?

_____

3. Where would you expect to find an **oasis**?

_____

4. Everyone says that Frances is **scowling.** What is Frances doing?

_____

5. What would you do with a **corral**?

_____

6. Karl weighs 130 pounds. Can he box as a **featherweight**?

_____

7. Lance received a **cobbler** for his birthday. What could he do with it?

_____

8. Juan is an **acrobat.** How can people tell?

_____

9. Ralph's family is going to a **lodge.** What should Ralph expect?

_____

10. What is a **palindrome**?

_____

Using Dictionary Entries

Directions Read the entry below. Then follow the directions.

> **eat** ('ēt) *v.* **ate** ('at, *chiefly Brit or substand* 'et); **eat•en** ('e-tɘ n); **eat•ing** [OE *etan*]
> *v.t.* **1:** to take in through the mouth as food: ingest, chew, and swallow in turn
> **2:** to destroy, consume, or waste by or as if by eating: DEVOUR (operating
> expenses *ate* up the profits) **3 a:** to consume gradually: CORRODE **b:** to consume
> with vexation: BOTHER (what's ~*ing* her now) —*v.i.* **1:** to take food or a meal
> **2:** to affect something by gradual destruction or consumption – usu. used with
> *into, away,* or *at* – **eat•er** *n.*

EXAMPLE   What is the noun form of the word *eat*? __eater_____

1. In the space provided, write the correct form of *eat*.

A Don't disturb the dog while he is _____.

B Yesterday I _____ chicken for dinner.

C Mary has _____ all of her lunch.

D Mother said the baby was a good _____ .

E Be sure to _____ your spinach!

2. From what language did *eat* come? _____

3. What is the root form of the word *eat*? _____

4. Which meaning of *eat* is used in the following sentences? In the space
provided, write the number (and letter if necessary) of each meaning.

_____   **A** The rust **ate** up the iron fence.

_____   **B** The moths **ate** a hole in my wool coat.

_____   **C** **Eat** your dinner.

_____   **D** You look upset. Is something **eating** you, Harry?

_____   **E** The locusts **ate** up the crops.

5. What part of speech is *eat*? _____

Using Dictionaries to Check Spelling

Directions: Write the plural of each word. You may use a dictionary to find the correct spelling.

EXAMPLE   puppy __puppies_____

---

1. alligator _____   **4.** umbrella _____

2. object _____   **5.** battery _____

3. enemy _____

Directions: Add *-ed* to form the past tense and *-ing* to form the present participle of each word. You may use a dictionary to find the correct spelling.

EXAMPLE   talk   **Past tense**   **Present participle**
A __talked_____   B __talking_____

		Past tense		**Present participle**
1. fry	A	_____	B	_____
2. crouch	A	_____	B	_____
3. owe	A	_____	B	_____

Directions: Circle the word that correctly completes each sentence. You may use a dictionary to find the correct spelling.

EXAMPLE   I live on the left side of the _____.
(A) road   **B** rode

---

1. May I go _____?
  A to   **B** too

2. This hat is on _____.
  A sale   **B** sail

Using Dictionaries to Find Facts

Directions: Use the entries below to answer the questions that follow.

Mao Tse-tung (ˈmau̇-(ʹ) (d)zə du̇ŋ) 1893–1976 Chinese communist leader

mar•a•thon (ˈmar- ə -ˌthän) *n.* [*Marathon*, Greece, site of a victory of Greeks over Persians in 490 B.C., the news of which was carried to Athens by a long-distance runner] **1:** a foot race of 26 miles, 385 yards **2:** any long-distance or endurance contest

Mar•di Gras (ˈmär-dē-ˌgrä) *n.* [Fr, lit., fat Tuesday] **1:** Shrove Tuesday, the last day before Lent **2:** a day of merrymaking and carnival (as in New Orleans) of marking the climax of a carnival period

Marie An•toi•nette (ˌan-twə-ʹnet, -tə -), 1755-1793 wife of Louis XVI; queen of France (1774–1792): executed by guillotine for treason

Mars (ˈmärz) *n.* **1:** *Rom. Myth.* the god of war—identified with the Greek Ares **2:** a personification of war **3:** a planet of the solar system

---

EXAMPLE   How old was Mao Tse-tung when he died? __83 years old_____

---

1. Of what country was Mao Tse-tung the leader? _____

2. Jack is running in a marathon next month. How many miles must he

   run to finish the race? _____

3. In what country was the ancient city of Marathon? _____

4. What does *Mardi Gras* mean in French? _____

5. When is *Mardi Gras* each year? _____

6. To whom was Marie Antoinette married? _____

7. Why was Marie Antoinette executed? _____

8. How old was Mao Tse-tung when Marie Antoinette died? _____

9. What planet is named after the Roman god of war? _____

10. With what is Mars identified? _____

Almanacs

Directions Use a term from the word box to correctly complete each
sentence. Write your answers on the lines provided.

astronomical	farm	general	search
before	figures	home	sports
CD-ROM	free	magazine	topics
CIA	front	once	year

EXAMPLE Two kinds of almanacs are farmer's almanacs and __general__
information almanacs.

1. An almanac is a book of facts published _____ a year.

2. Almanacs contain facts and _____.

3. A farmer's almanac includes an annual calendar, weather predictions,
   and _____ facts.

4. A farmer's almanac provides other information helpful for _____ and home care.

5. You can use an almanac's index to find the _____ an almanac covers.

6. Unlike most reference books, the index of an almanac is in the _____ of the book.

7. You might find _____ facts in a general information almanac.

8. An almanac often has facts about the year _____ its title date.

9. To find the most current information, you can use a publication such as a _____.

10. Electronic almanacs are on _____ or at an Internet Web site.

11. Electronic almanacs are usually _____.

12. The index of an electronic almanac usually appears on its _____ page.

13. You can find an electronic almanac by conducting a _____ using the word *almanac*.

14. You should check the _____ of an electronic almanac.

15. The _____ has a reliable online almanac.

Atlases

Directions Circle the letter of the word that correctly completes each sentence.

1. You can use a(n) _____ to measure distances on a map.
   - **A** symbol
   - **B** grid
   - **C** atlas
   - **D** scale

2. To use a map, you must understand the _____, or pictures that represent things.
   - **A** grid
   - **B** atlas
   - **C** symbols
   - **D** scales

3. A(n) _____ is a book of maps.
   - **A** symbol
   - **B** gazetteer
   - **C** atlas
   - **D** scale

4. A _____ contains both numbers and letters to identify places.
   - **A** symbol
   - **B** grid map
   - **C** vertical
   - **D** gazetteer

5. A dictionary of geographical place names is called a(n) _____.
   - **A** grid map
   - **B** gazetteer
   - **C** map
   - **D** atlas

6. Lines going up and down on a map are _____.
   - **A** symbols
   - **B** scale
   - **C** horizontal
   - **D** vertical

7. Lines going across a map are _____.
   - **A** symbols
   - **B** scale
   - **C** horizontal
   - **D** vertical

8. A(n) _____ is made up of horizontal and vertical lines.
   - **A** gazetteer
   - **B** grid map
   - **C** scale
   - **D** atlas

9. You can find the location of a place by looking at a _____.
   - **A** scale
   - **B** gazetteer
   - **C** symbol
   - **D** map

10. A network of lines on a map that makes it possible to locate specific places is called a(n) _____.
    - **A** atlas
    - **B** search engine
    - **C** grid
    - **D** grid map

Maps

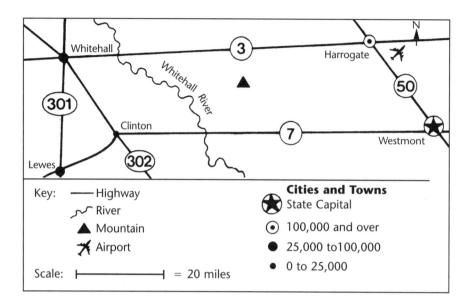

Directions: Answer these questions about the map above.

EXAMPLE   What road would you travel from the capital city to Harrogate?   **Highway 50** _____

---

1. Name two highways that go over the Whitehall River.

_____

2. Name the highway that connects Lewes and Whitehall.

_____

3. Name the highway that connects Lewes and Clinton.

_____

4. Name the roads that you would travel to go from Lewes to the airport.

_____

5. Name the two towns that are connected by Highway 302.

_____

6. How many miles would you travel to go from Westmont to Whitehall?

_____

7. What roads would you travel if you drove from Whitehall to the capital city?

_____

8. Which highways run east and west?

_____

9. If you started at the capital city and drove north, to what town would you be going?

_____

10. Name the largest town that is southwest of the airport.

_____

Encyclopedias

Part A For each group of words, write the main topic you would search for in an encyclopedia.

EXAMPLE   poodles, schnauzers, _dogs_____ , spaniels

1. shirt, pants, clothes, socks _____

2. planes, cars, trucks, transportation _____

3. music, guitar, song, piano _____

4. green, colors, blue, beige _____

5. computer, DVD, technology, CD-ROM_____

Part B Thinking of subtopics related to main topics can help you search for information in an encyclopedia. Write a main topic for each subtopic listed below.

EXAMPLE   **Subtopic:** carpet
Main topic: _flooring_____

1. Subtopic: drums

   Main topic: _____

2. Subtopic: lipstick

   Main topic: _____

3. Subtopic: novel

   Main topic: _____

4. Subtopic: stove

   Main topic: _____

5. Subtopic: bowl

   Main topic: _____

Cookbooks

Abbreviation:	Stands for:	Equivalent to:
c	cup.	8 ounces
doz	dozen.	12 units
F.	Fahrenheit (a measure of heat)	
g.	gram	$\frac{1}{28}$ of an ounce
hr.	hour	60 minutes
lb.	pound	16 dry ounces
min.	minute	60 seconds
oz.	ounce.	$\frac{1}{16}$ of a pound; $\frac{1}{8}$ of a cup
pkg.	package (container)	
pt.	pint	16 fluid ounces
qt.	quart	32 fluid ounces
t., tsp	teaspoon (a unit of liquid or dry measure)	$\frac{1}{3}$ of a tablespoon
T., tbsp.	tablespoon (a unit of liquid or dry measure)	3 teaspoons

Directions Use the recipe information above to answer the following questions.

> **EXAMPLE**   How many ounces make up a cup? __8__

1. How many pints do you need to make a quart? _____

2. Write two ways to abbreviate *teaspoon.* _____

3. What is the abbreviation for *pound*? _____

4. How many cups are in a pint? _____

5. How many ounces make up a quart? _____

6. What is the abbreviation for *ounce*? _____

7. A cake is to bake at 350° F. What does *F* mean? _____

8. How many teaspoons equal one tablespoon? _____

9. A recipe calls for $\frac{1}{2}$ dozen eggs. How many eggs do you need? _____

10. A stew should simmer for one hour and a half. How many minutes does that equal? _____

11. How much larger is an ounce than a gram? _____

12. Which is larger—a pint or a cup? _____

13. Which is smaller—a teaspoon or a tablespoon? _____

14. Which is larger—a quart or a pint? _____

15. How many ounces make up a pint? _____

Food Labels

Directions Read the information on these two labels. Then answer the questions.

EXAMPLE   How many servings are in one container of the granola bars? __8__

Granola Bars
Orchard Blend
Nutrition Facts
Serving Size: 1 bar (28g)
Servings Per Container 8

Amount Per Serving	
Calories	110
Calories from Fat	15

	% Daily Value*
Total Fat 2g	3%
Saturated Fat 0g	0%
Cholesterol 0mg	0%
Sodium 65mg	3%
Total Carbohydrate 21g	7%
Dietary Fiber 1g	5%
Sugars 8g	
Protein 2g	
Iron	2%
Thiamin	2%

Not a significant source of vitamin A, vita-min C and calcium.
*Percent daily values are based on a 2,000 calorie diet. Your daily values might be higher or lower depending on your calorie needs

Calories		2000	2500
Total Fat	Less than	65g	80g
Sat Fat	Less than	20g	25g
Cholesterol	Less than	300mg	300mg
Sodium	Less than	2400mg	2400mg
Total Carbohydrate		300g	375g
Dietary Fiber		25g	30g

INGREDIENTS: ROLLED OATS, CORN SYRUP, CRISP RICE (RICE FLOUR, RICE BRAN, MALT), BROWN SUGAR, RAISINS, HIGH FRUCTOSE CORN SYRUP, SUN-FLOWER OIL, SUGAR, MALTODEXTRIN, *APPLES (COLOR PRESERVED BY SODIUM SULFITE), GLYC-ERIN, HONEY, FRUCTOSE, *CORN SYRUP, CRANBERRIES, APPLE JUICE CONCENTRATE, BROWN SUGAR SYRUP, NONFAT MILK, SALT, NATURAL FLAVOR, BAKING SODA, SOY LECITHIN, ALMOND PIECES, SPICE.
*DRIED

Chicken Broth

Nutrition Facts	**As Soup**	**In Recipes**
Serving Size:	1 cup (240mL)	½ cup (120mL)
Servings Per Container	About 2	About 3.5

Amount Per Serving		
Calories	15	10
	% Daily Value*	% Daily Value*
Total Fat 0g+, 0g++	0%	0%
Sodium 560mg, 280mg	23%	12%
Total Carb. 1g, Less Than 1g	0%	0%
Sugars 1g, Less Than 1g		
Protein 3g, 1g		

Not a significant source of calories from fat, saturated fat, cholesterol, dietary fiber, vitamin A, vitamin C, calcium and iron.

+Amount in Soup   ++ Amount in Recipes
*Percent Daily Values are based on a 2,000 calorie diet.
INGREDIENTS: CHICKEN BROTH, SALT, CHICKEN FLAVOR (CONTAINS AUTOLYZED YEAST), DEXTROSE, CORN SYRUP SOLIDS AND SPICE EXTRACT.

1. What is the main ingredient in the granola bars?

_____

2. What is the second ingredient in the chicken broth?

_____

3. Which food has more sodium per serving—the granola bars

or the chicken broth as soup? _____

4. Which food has less fat per serving? _____

5. Which food has more carbohydrates per serving? _____

6. Which food contains less than 4% of the Daily Value of iron per serving? _____

7. Which food has more calories per serving? _____

8. Which items under Nutrition Facts are measured in milligrams? _____

9. How is the serving size of the chicken broth measured? _____

10. How is the serving size of the granola bars measured? _____

How-to Books

Directions Read the list of book titles below. Circle the titles that name how-to books. Cross out the titles that do not name how-to books.

1. *Kitchen Science Experiments*

2. *How Grass Grows*

3. *The Green Monster of Abbeyville*

4. *Police Training 101*

5. *My Favorite Aliens*

6. *Carpentry for Beginners*

7. *The Magic Treasure Chest*

8. *Samson, the Talking Dog*

9. *How to Care for Yorkshire Terriers*

10. *My Favorite Movie Star*

11. *Law School Success Guide*

12. *Getting into the College of Your Choice*

13. *Ceramics Made Easy*

14. *Giving Effective Speeches*

15. *Patty's Lost Coin*

Magazines

Directions Read each clue. Fill in the blanks with the word that matches each clue. Then solve the acrostic phrase.

(**EXAMPLE**) once a month

<u>m</u> <u>o</u> <u>n</u> <u>t</u> <u>h</u> <u>l</u> <u>y</u>

---

1. twice a month

___ ___ ___ ___ ___ ___ ___ ___ ___
14 13 2 18 15 9 16 3 1

2. once a day

___ ___ ___ ___ ___
4 12 13 3 1

3. yearly

___ ___ ___ ___ ___ ___ ___ ___
12 15 15 5 12 3 3 1

4. every week

___ ___ ___ ___ ___ ___
10 11 11 16 3 1

5. the space of time between events

___ ___ ___ ___ ___ ___ ___ ___
13 15 9 11 17 6 12 3

6. a period of time needed for an event to repeat itself

___ ___ ___ ___ ___
8 1 8 3 11

7. a magazine published at regular intervals

___ ___ ___ ___ ___ ___ ___ ___ ___ ___
19 11 17 13 18 4 13 8 12 3

8. twice a year

___ ___ ___ ___ ___ ___ ___ ___ ___ ___
14 13 12 15 15 5 12 3 3 1

9. twice a month

___ ___ ___ ___ ___ ___ ___ ___ ___
14 13 2 18 15 9 16 3 1

10. a magazine that contains summaries or condensed articles from other magazines

___ ___ ___ ___ ___ ___
4 13 21 11 14 9

Acrostic Phrase

___ ___ ___ ___   ___ ___ ___   ___ ___ ___ ___   ___ ___ ___ ___ ___
9 13 2 11   12 15 4   9 13 2 11   12 21 12 13 15

Magazine Facts

Part A Fill out the magazine subscription form below completely. Order the magazine for one year.

SPORTS CAR DIGEST
Discount Prices

Mail this discount card today and you will receive *Sports Car Digest* at only $2.00 an issue—a 50% savings off the cover price.

❑ 1 year   ❑ 18 months   ❑ 2 years   ❑ Check enclosed
  (52 issues)   (78 issues)   (104 issues)   ❑ Bill me later

Mr. ❑ / Ms. ❑ _____

Address _____

City _____ State _____ Zip _____

(PRINT IN INK, PLEASE)

Part B Match each word in the first column with its meanings in the second column. Write the correct letters on the lines provided.

Words	Meanings
_____ **1.** annually	**A** twice a month
_____ **2.** interval	**B** a magazine published at regular intervals, such as daily or weekly
_____ **3.** monthly	**C** the period of time needed for a certain event to repeat itself
_____ **4.** cycle	**D** once a month
_____ **5.** periodical	**E** once a year
_____ **6.** daily	**F** once a day
_____ **7.** bimonthly	**G** a space of time between events
_____ **8.** publish	**H** to print and distribute magazines, books, or other materials
_____ **9.** condensed	**I** a regular order for a magazine
_____ **10.** subscription	**J** a shorter version of an article

Telephone Books

Directions Write these names in alphabetical order the way they would appear in a telephone directory.

EXAMPLE

Wilson's Best Buys
Wilton's Telephone Repairs
Walker, April L
A Walker

Walker A _____
Walker, April L _____
Wilson's Best Buys _____
Wilton's Telephone Repairs _____

WWDC–AM 1200 _____

WWDC–TV 6 _____

A L Walker _____

City of Wilkinson _____

The Wall: Paint and Paper _____

Wallpaper, Inc. _____

April and Dave Walker _____

W & R Sportswear _____

R L Woodmore _____

Jean and Ray Woodmore _____

Directions Match each name in List One with a name in the Alternative Spelling list. Write the letter of your answers on the lines provided.

EXAMPLE

B	Morrison	**A** Pearlman
D	Kaufman	**B** Morison
E	Summerville	**C** McKinney
C	MacKinney	**D** Coffman
A	Perlman	**E** Sommerville

	List One		**Alternative Spelling**
_____	**1.** Paige	**A**	Greene
_____	**2.** Green	**B**	Kohn
_____	**3.** Rodgers	**C**	Page
_____	**4.** Cohn	**D**	Ackermann
_____	**5.** Ackerman	**E**	Rogers

 Life Skills English

Using Telephone Books

Directions On the lines provided, answer the questions below. Use this sample from the Yellow Pages.

210 Detective - Diamonds

OVER 15 YEARS EXPERIENCE
INVESTIGATIONS
COVERING THE ENTIRE U.S.A
• INSURANCE • CRIMINAL • CIVIL
• DIVORCE • MISSING PERSONS
TRAINED ARMED BODY GUARDS
Freedom Security Investigation
Bob Smith   **777-6111**
Director   102 OVERBROOK AVE

MICHAELS & DANIELS
INVESTIGATION SERVICE
★ BONDED ★
LICENSED BY STATE POLICE
DIVORCE & CHILD CUSTODY SPECIALISTS
All matters are confidential
867-1294   **CHARLES TOWERS**
              MELWOOD

Detective Agencies (cont'd)
NATIONAL DETECTIVE AGENCY INC
20 YEARS OF SATISFIED SERVICE
UNIFORMED GUARDS
WATCHMEN SERVICE
PROTECTION SPECIALISTS
REASONABLE RATES
24-HR SERVICE
RADIO PATROL CAR
998-6340
19 W Falls Road

Diamonds
ARTIST JEWELERS
"We specialize in diamond jewelry"
NorthEast Mall ---------------- **917-6211**
Center City -------------------- **315-6488**
BERNET'S 13 N Preston Av--------- **411-8229**
BLOCKMAN'S JEWELRY
WE WILL CUSTOM DESIGN
3102 Calver Av --------------- **848-7221**

EXAMPLE Which detective agency offers 24-hour service?   **National Detective Agency Inc**

1. Which detective agency is licensed by the state police?   _____

2. For which detective agency does Bob Smith work?   _____

3. Which detective agency would you recommend to a friend with child custody problems?   _____

4. What is the address of Bernet's?   _____

5. From which dealer could you buy custom jewelry?   _____

The Yellow Pages list businesses by subject. The White Pages list the names of professional people and businesses in alphabetical order.

Directions Read these situations. Decide whether you need to use the Yellow Pages or the White Pages. Circle your answer.

EXAMPLE Carl needs a dentist appointment. He plans to call Dr. Joseph Keller.   Yellow   (White)

1. Mickey can't remember the telephone number of his high school. He needs to call the counselor.   Yellow   White

2. Brenda's television is broken. She heard that Powley's TV Repair is reliable.   Yellow   White

3. Ray wants to find a place near his house to play golf.   Yellow   White

4. Dave wants to frame a picture as a birthday gift for his mother. He needs to know when the Frame Shop is open.   Yellow   White

5. The Frame Shop is not open any evenings. Dave needs to find another store near his house with evening hours.   Yellow   White

Telephone Numbers

Directions Use the sample telephone book page to find the answers
to the questions below. Write your answers on the lines provided.

COOKE—COOPER   **348**

Cooke Thomas C & Mary 141 Cylburn Av 490-1800	Cook's Barber Shop 2709 Chesterfield Av 285-5594
Cooke Thomas G 29 Arbor Court 338-0563	Cook's Hardware 3507 Baker St 566-3200
Cooke W H Co Inc 6317 N Charles St 761-2299	Cooney John B Jr 106 Falls Rd 276-7450
Cooke Wilbur 920 Keswick Rd 848-7943	Cooney John B Sr 4222 Elmley Av 377-8577
Cooke William H Jr 2 E North Av 664-4009	Cooney Lois R 3901 Wise Av 675-1081
Cooke William H Sr 9307 Maine Av 795-9253	Cooper A 148 Brendan Ct 252-1097
Cookerly Glen H 2301 Park Heights Av 490-0561	Cooper A 10163 Maryland Av 647-0207
Cookie Shop 938 N Gilmore 358-2442	Cooper Allan 1700 28th St 725-2120
	Cooper Arthur
Cook's Allied Discount Stores—	1000 Richards Rd Fallston 792-0395
2745 Gyro Dr 574-3838	Cooper Arthur
5816 Cold Spring La 879-8627	Fallston . . . Harford Rd Tel No 866-2805
9203 Round Rd 557-9832	Cooper Barry 1563 Oak St 744-6909

EXAMPLE   What are the guide words for this sample page?   **Cooke, Cooper**

---

1. What is the telephone number of Wilbur Cooke?

_____

2. How many people with the last name *Cooke* are listed on this page?

_____

3. If you wanted to make an appointment for a haircut, what number could you dial?

_____

4. If you wanted to call William H. Cooke's son, what number would you dial?

_____

5. What is the telephone number of the Cook's store located on Cold Spring Lane?

_____

6. Where does the father of John B. Cooney, Jr. live?

_____

7. What is the telephone number of A. Cooper who lives on Maryland Avenue?

_____

8. What person is listed before Lois Cooney?

_____

9. On what page would the name of Charles Cooper appear?

_____

10. What is Arthur Cooper's address in Fallston?

_____

Telephone Service Providers and Bills

Directions Match each word in the first column with its meaning in the second column. Write the correct letters on the lines provided.

(**EXAMPLE**) ___A___ DSL   **A** provides faster Internet service

Words

_____ **1.** telephone service provider

_____ **2.** automatic callback

_____ **3.** caller ID

_____ **4.** call forwarding

_____ **5.** voice mail

_____ **6.** ISP

_____ **7.** enhanced repeat dialing

_____ **8.** basic telephone service

_____ **9.** optional telephone service

_____ **10.** call waiting

Meanings

A records messages of incoming calls

B additional telephone functions for a fee

C redials busy phone numbers

D tells you that you have another call

E most simple phone service

F sends recorded calls to another phone

G provides telephone services

H calls back last incoming call

I shows name and number of person calling

J connects computers to the Internet

Cell Phones and Phone Cards

Directions Circle *T* for true or *F* for false for each of the following statements. Then rewrite each false statement to make it true.

EXAMPLE   T (F) Cell phones and phone cards are large and difficult to carry.
Cell phones and phone cards are small and easy to carry.

T F **1.** Cell phones operate by telephone lines.

T F **2.** Phone cards are prepaid long distance cards.

T F **3.** A phone card can be used like a charge card.

T F **4.** You can send and receive calls on a cell phone.

T F **5.** Cell phones work well in all areas.

T F **6.** You can use a cell phone in an emergency.

T F **7.** Cell phones do not need batteries to work.

T F **8.** Cell phone companies offer long-distance services.

T F **9.** You cannot call long distance with a phone card.

T F **10.** You can buy a prepaid phone card at many stores.

What's in a Library?

Directions Choose a term from the box that each sentence describes.
Write the term on the line provided after each sentence.

compact discs (CDs)	magazines	telephone books
digital video discs (DVDs)	newspapers	videotapes
guides	paperback books	
hardback books	reference books	

EXAMPLE   These materials can include movies or other productions on tape.
     videotapes

1. These can store music or computer information.

_____

2. Libraries subscribe to these, which are most often published monthly.

_____

3. These can include fiction and nonfiction books that have durable bindings.

_____

4. These provide information about colleges and vocational schools.

_____

5. These can store much more information than videotapes.

_____

6. You can use these to find local addresses and phone numbers.

_____

7. These are softcover books that you can check out from the library.

_____

8. You can find current information on a daily basis in these.

_____

9. These include documentaries and training programs that are played in a VCR.

_____

10. These include atlases, encyclopedias, and dictionaries.

_____

Fiction Books

Directions Arrange these fiction books in the order that they would appear on a shelf in a library. Write them in order on the lines provided.

The Adventures of Tom Sawyer by Mark Twain

The Outsiders by S. E. Hinton

Watership Down by Richard Adams

Robinson Crusoe by Daniel Defoe

The Clan of the Cave Bear by Jean Auel

The Valley of the Horses by Jean Auel

Bleak House by Charles Dickens

A Tale of Two Cities by Charles Dickens

Penrod by Booth Tarkington

Exodus by Leon Uris

Book of Lights by Chaim Potok

Rebecca of Sunnybrook Farm by Kate Douglas Wiggins

Show Boat by Edna Ferber

Murder at the Vicarage by Agatha Christie

The Living Reed by Pearl Buck

EXAMPLE The first five are done for you.

---

1. **Watership Down** by Richard Adams

2. **The Clan of the Cave Bear** by Jean Auel

3. **The Valley of the Horses** by Jean Auel

4. **The Living Reed** by Pearl Buck

5. **Murder at the Vicarage** by Agatha Christie

6. _____

7. _____

8. _____

9. _____

10. _____

11. _____

12. _____

13. _____

14. _____

15. _____

The Dewey Decimal System

Directions For each book title, circle the letter of the category in which you would find the book.

EXAMPLE
Information Please Almanac
(A) 000–099 General Works   **C** 700–799 Arts and Recreation
B 500–599 Pure Sciences   **D** 900–999 History and Geography

---

1. The Life of Dolly Madison
   A 000–099 General Works   **C** 500–599 Pure Sciences
   B 200–299 Religion   **D** 900–999 History and Geography

2. Managing Your Self-Esteem
   A 000–099 General Works   **C** 200–299 Religion
   B 100–199 Philosophy and Psychology   **D** 300–399 Social Sciences

3. Radio-Controlled Boats
   A 600–699 Technology (Applied Sciences)   **C** 800–899 Literature
   B 400–499 Language   **D** 900–999 History and Geography

4. The Paintings of Picasso
   A 300–399 Social Sciences   **C** 700–799 Arts and Recreation
   B 500–599 Pure Sciences   **D** 800–899 Literature

5. The Works of Charles Dickens
   A 100–199 Philosophy and Psychology   **C** 800–899 Literature
   B 300–399 Social Sciences   **D** 900–999 History and Geography

6. Diagramming Sentences
   A 200–299 Religion   **C** 400–499 Language
   B 300–399 Social Sciences   **D** 500–599 Pure Sciences

7. French for Beginners
   A 300–399 Social Sciences   **C** 700–799 Arts and Recreation
   B 400–499 Language   **D** 800–899 Literature

8. Martin Luther King's Speeches
   A 000–099 General Works   **C** 700–799 Arts and Recreation
   B 100–199 Philosophy and Psychology   **D** 800–899 Literature

9. Hebrew Rites and Passages
   A 200–299 Religion   **C** 700–799 Arts and Recreation
   B 400–499 Language   **D** 800–899 Literature

10. The Anatomy of a Frog
   A 100–199 Philosophy and Psychology   **C** 500–599 Pure Sciences
   B 400–499 Language   **D** 900–999 History and Geography

Using the Dewey Decimal System

Here are the main headings and numbers of the Dewey Decimal System.

000–099	General Works	500s	Pure Sciences
100s	Philosophy and Psychology	600s	Technology (Applied Sciences)
200s	Religion	700s	Arts and Recreation
300s	Social Sciences	800s	Literature
400s	Language	900s	History and Geography

Directions Read the book titles below. For each book, write the number for the category of the Dewey Decimal System on the lines provided.

EXAMPLE _____400s_____ *Webster's New World Dictionary*

_____ **1.** *The World Almanac*

_____ **2.** *The Bible Story Book*

_____ **3.** *The World of the Past*

_____ **4.** *My Life* by Golda Meir

_____ **5.** *Mythology* by Edith Hamilton

_____ **6.** *The World of Poetry*

_____ **7.** *Basic Car Repair*

_____ **8.** *The Complete Book of Garden Magic*

_____ **9.** *Beginning German*

_____ **10.** *Introduction to Computer Science*

_____ **11.** *Short Stories of Edgar Allan Poe*

_____ **12.** *The Miracle of Language*

_____ **13.** *Better Tennis*

_____ **14.** *Hammond's Atlas*

_____ **15.** *The Judy Collins Songbook*

_____ **16.** *Elvis Presley*

_____ **17.** *200 Popular Jokes*

_____ **18.** *Introduction to Mathematics*

_____ **19.** *Betty Crocker's Picture Cookbook*

_____ **20.** *Football Today*

Periodicals and Audiovisuals

Directions For each of the following statements, circle *T* for true or *F* for false. Then rewrite each false statement to make it true.

EXAMPLE   T Ⓕ   Libraries subscribe to every magazine that is published.
Libraries do not subscribe to every magazine that is published.

T   F   **1.** Libraries offer current issues and back issues of magazines.

_____

T   F   **2.** Most libraries display back issues of periodicals on shelves.

_____

T   F   **3.** You can find magazine topics by looking in an atlas.

_____

T   F   **4.** Most libraries allow people to check out magazines.

_____

T   F   **5.** Many periodicals are published every day.

_____

T   F   **6.** A current issue of a magazine is the most recent issue.

_____

T   F   **7.** Libraries arrange videos on the shelf by category.

_____

T   F   **8.** All of the issues of one magazine make a volume.

_____

T   F   **9.** A documentary is about imaginary people and places.

_____

T   F   **10.** Magazines and periodicals are the same thing.

_____

Finding Information in a Library

Directions Read the following statements. If the statement is true, write
True on the line provided. If the statement is not true, write *False*.

EXAMPLE   **True** _____ A reference section is a specific area of a library that has
encyclopedias, catalogs, maps, and dictionaries.

_____ **1.** Most libraries have switched from computer catalogs to card catalogs.

_____ **2.** The Dewey Decimal number appears on the back of each nonfiction book.

_____ **3.** A computer record in the library's catalog provides information about how
to locate an item in the library.

_____ **4.** Any book you find in the reference section of the library can be checked out.

_____ **5.** A vertical file can contain pamphlets and other materials too large to fit on
a library shelf.

_____ **6.** The library's catalog will not tell you at which branch the material is located.

_____ **7.** To find a book in the library using a computer, you need to know the book's
call number.

_____ **8.** The letters *YA* on the back of a nonfiction book mean it is noncirculating.

_____ **9.** To search the computer catalog by a book's author, you type the last name
first, followed by a comma, and then the first name.

_____ **10.** The letters *F* or *FIC* sometimes label nonfiction books.

Television

Here is an example of a daily television schedule published in the newspaper.

	4	5	7	9	20	26
7:00	Harry's House	Our Story	Can You Beat This!	Spin the Wheel	Love of Your Life	Fix It Up
7:30	Doctors	Fronier Family	Win Big!			Woodworking World
8:00	Alex & Jill	MOVIE: A REAL		Crime Stories	Phil	Market Tonight
8:30	Doctors				Buster's Blues	
9:00	Courtroom		College Football: Smallville U at Lincolnburg	Lawyers	Neighbors	Travels in China
9:30					One Great Summer	

EXAMPLE What time does "Spin the Wheel" start? __7:00__

1. How many channels are listed? _____

2. What time does "Harry's House" end on Channel 4? _____

3. Which channel carries "Market Tonight"? _____

4. At what time does "Frontier Family" end? _____

5. What channel carries "Crime Stories"? _____

6. At what time does the movie "A Real Adventure" begin on Channel 5? _____

7. What programs occupy the 7:00 to 8:00 time slot on Channel 26? _____

8. How many channels feature full-length movies? _____

9. What channel carries "Buster's Blues"? _____

10. What college football teams can be seen on Channel 7? _____

Radio

Directions Use the correct term from the box to complete each sentence. Terms may be used more than once.

Federal Communications Commission format   multimedia playlist tape-delayed

EXAMPLE   Another word for radio program style is <u>format</u>.

1. Scheduled music that a radio station plays is a _____.

2. The abbreviation *FCC* stands for _____.

3. _____ is a combination of television, radio, newspaper, magazines, and the Internet.

4. A program that is recorded and played later is _____.

5. You can check a radio station's _____ to find out what music they will be playing.

6. The _____ provides licenses for radio stations to operate.

7. A radio program that is not live, but taped is _____.

8. Today, many large radio stations are owned and operated by

_____ companies.

9. Radio stations design a particular _____ so that they can reach their goal to inform, persuade, or entertain.

10. The _____ decides how much airtime radio stations can sell to commercial advertisers.

Newspapers

Directions Use the newspaper index to answer the questions below. Write the name of the section, its letter, and the page number on the lines below each question.

Index		
Classified C18	Local. C1	Sports D1
Comics B24	Movies B13	Television B16
Editorials A15	National and World . . A1	
Food B1	Obituaries. C10	

EXAMPLE You want to find a used bike. Where would you look?

      Classified   **C**   **18**

---

1. In which section would you look for a help-wanted ad?

_____ _____ _____

2. Which section would have your favorite comic strip?

_____ _____ _____

3. Is a rerun of your favorite show on? Where would you look?

_____ _____ _____

4. Where might you find a recipe for potato salad?

_____ _____ _____

5. Where would you look to find out when a movie begins?

_____ _____ _____

6. Where would you find out the time of a funeral?

_____ _____ _____

7. Which section would have the paper's opinion of an event?

_____ _____ _____

8. Where would you find a report on the president's speech?

_____ _____ _____

9. Where would you find an article about a new park in your town?

_____ _____ _____

10. Where would you find the scores of last night's baseball games?

_____ _____ _____

Advertisements

Advertisments try to persuade consumers that the product or service being sold is the best for them.

Directions Study each ad. Answer the questions that follow each ad.

EXAMPLE   Where would you go to buy a California pita sandwich?
1616 Broadway _____

MIKE'S
DISCOUNT TELEVISIONS
View Your Favorite
Programs for Less!
555-9911
3010 Booker Street

1. What is the phone number for this business?

_____

2. Where is this business?

_____

3. What is the business's slogan?

_____

PICTURE THIS...

A BRAND NEW SEDAN
FOR $14,500
EVERYTHING IS INCLUDED IN PRICE
MUST SELL TO MAKE ROOM FOR OTHER CARS
NO TRICKS! NO GIMMICKS!

6. What is the price of the car shown in this advertisement?

_____

7. Is the car advertised new or used?

_____

8. Why does the ad say this car must be sold?

_____

SHOP ANTON'S FASHION SALON
FOR THE LATEST IN
FALL FASHIONS
We have a collection of the newest and best in suits, blouses, and dresses.
1108 Central St.
"TO BE WITH IT, BE WITH US"

4. What items of clothing are sold at this business?

_____

5. What is the name of this business?

_____

FOR THE FIRST TIME ON THE
EAST COAST!
 The *real* California pita
sandwich
★ $1.00 off a pita sandwich ★
with this ad
CALL FOR PICK-UP ORDERS
1616 Broadway ------------------------- 555-9606

9. What do you have to do to get $1.00 off a pita sandwich?

_____

10. What should you do to place a pick-up order?

_____

Classified Ads

Directions Write the abbreviation for each term below. (You may refer to
"Abbreviations Used in Automobile Advertisements" on page 188 of your
textbook.) Then find each abbreviation in the puzzle. The words go up,
down, across, backward, and diagonally.

EXAMPLE   excellent condition   **excl/cond** _____

---

1. air conditioned   _____

2. sunroof   _____

3. engine   _____

4. AM/FM radio   _____

5. cassette tape player   _____

6. rear window defroster   _____

7. automatic transmission   _____

8. convertible   _____

9. low mileage   _____

10. power   _____

```
S Y D L L R C A N R F I U Y R
C D O M T F A V U R I F N C U
M M Q J K E S P N T M A D G Z
I V W D G D S U O F O N B O J
D G C T Y R S B F C G E V R N
U U R Z B A C O D O N F U B E
K H Q P S E V Z Z W E Z A Q S
Z O N U B R N F D Y H X J Q L
C Z J U V Z R Z J A R I F C U
C U Z T V W A B G E P U E K F
C O N V P D O E N Q Z N Y J D
E V M R A M F M A A V G Z N R
V U K E J P B J N D Q D U T U
Z V H M C A K K V I A H K I D
P P Q X O B I E X C L C O N D
```

Help-Wanted Ads

Part A Help-wanted ads use abbreviations to save space. Match the abbreviations in the left-hand column with the terms in the right-hand column. Write the correct letter before each abbreviation.

Abbreviations	Terms
_____ **1.** exp. or exp'd	**A** excellent
_____ **2.** sal.	**B** thousand
_____ **3.** oppty.	**C** appointment
_____ **4.** K	**D** between
_____ **5.** exc.	**E** preferred
_____ **6.** pref.	**F** Equal Opportunity Employer
_____ **7.** betw.	**G** experienced
_____ **8.** EOE	**H** with
_____ **9.** w/	**I** opportunity
_____ **10.** appt.	**J** salary

Part B Find the abbreviations in the following ads. Then write the full terms on the corresponding numbered lines below.

HELP WANTED (400)
1. DELI PERSON—Full time. Exp. only need apply. Call for an interview 555-5812.
2. DENTAL ASSISTANT Full time. A good oppty avail. in an establ., quality group practice in Towson. 1 evening per wk. no weekends. 555-4826.
3. DENTAL ASSISTANT Specialty prac. Pikeville area. X-ray certified, pref. exp'd only 555-2544.

HELP WANTED (400)
4. DENTAL HYGIENIST—Part time for Columbus office. Immed. openings. 555-1344 or 555-9172.
5. DENTAL HYGIENIST needed. Half day, alternate Sat. Exc. sal. Pleasant relaxed office. 555-2722.
6. DENTAL HYGIENIST Part Time exp. Belmont area, call wkdays 555-8189.
7. DENTAL RECEPTIONIST 4 days. Downtown. Nice office 555-6137 aft. 6.

HELP WANTED (400)
8. DENTAL TECHNICIAN Part time. Partial & denture exp. Send resume & salary requirements to Box MM48711.
9. DENTAL/OFFICE CLERK Part time Mon thru Fri, 15–20 hrs per wk. Dental insurance claim experience required. Towson 555-4229.
10. ELECTRICIAN w/industrial experience. For appt call 555-8550 EOE.

1. _____ 6. _____

2. _____ 7. _____

3. _____ 8. _____

4. _____ 9. _____

5. _____ 10. _____

Reading Help-Wanted Ads

Directions Read the help-wanted ads. Then answer the questions below.

FURNITURE FINISHER — (two positions) 40 hrs. a week. Mon. thru Fri. $7.50 per hr. Dawson Employment Agency. 1140 West Turner Blvd.

GENERAL OFFICE WORKER — Real estate. Good typist, mature. Salary determined by ability. Reply Daily Banner, Box Number 0040.

LANDSCAPE LABORERS — Exper. pref. No grass cutting. Must have own car. Call with refs. & their phone numbers, between 8 A.M. and 4 P.M. only. 555-3020.

MANAGER — Sylvia's. Ladies specialty shop is seeking mature, exper. assistant & manager trainees. Excel. co. benefits & good working conditions. Call Mrs. Wilson, 555-9030.

MESSENGER— Must own bicycle, part-time A.M., 2 hrs./day, 5 day wk. $80. 555-0900.

OFFICE CLEANERS — Experienced in floor care. Part time, 6 P.M.–10 P.M.—Monday to Friday. 555-8920.

EXAMPLE How many furniture finishers are needed? **two**

1. How many hours per week will the messenger work? _____

2. How much will the messenger be paid per hour? _____

3. How many hours per week will the office cleaners work? _____

4. For which job must the worker have a car? _____

5. In what kind of business will the general office worker be employed? _____

6. What does "salary determined by ability" mean? _____

7. For which jobs must the worker have experience? _____

8. How much will the furniture finisher earn per week? _____

9. The ad for manager promises good benefits.
   Write two benefits you might expect to receive in this position.

   _____

   _____

10. Two ads do not include telephone numbers.
    Explain how you would apply for each of these jobs.

    _____

    _____

Professionals

Directions Match each medical professional in Column A with the area of special training in Column B. Write the letter of your answer on the line provided. Use a dictionary if necessary.

EXAMPLE   ___A___ chiropractor   **A** spinal column

Column A

_____ **1.** dermatologist

_____ **2.** internist

_____ **3.** obstetrician

_____ **4.** orthopedist

_____ **5.** ophthalmologist

_____ **6.** pediatrician

_____ **7.** surgeon

_____ **8.** psychiatrist

_____ **9.** otolaryngologist

_____ **10.** podiatrist

_____ **11.** dentist

_____ **12.** oral surgeon

_____ **13.** periodontist

_____ **14.** gastroenterologist

_____ **15.** neurologist

Column B

A general surgery (operations)

B nervous or mental disorders

C infants and children

D skin disorders

E ear, nose, and throat

F bones, joints, and muscles

G eyes

H diseases that do not require surgery

I feet

J stomach and intestines

K surgery involving teeth

L gum disease

M brain and nervous system

N delivery of babies

O teeth

Help from Other Experts

Directions Read each situation. Choose the expert from the list that you would contact for each situation. Write the name of the expert on the line provided.

accountant	banker	librarian	travel agent
architect	cabinetmaker	pharmacist	veterinarian
attorney	electrician	plumber	

EXAMPLE   You need help planning a vacation. You could contact the __travel agent__.

1. You want to make a will. You want someone to advise you and to write the will. You could contact the _____.

2. The tax laws have changed again. You are having problems trying to prepare your income taxes. You could contact the

_____.

3. In your kitchen you have wooden cupboards. One of the doors needs to be replaced. You cannot find one at the hardware store that matches exactly. You could contact the

_____.

4. Your dog isn't eating. He lies around whimpering all day. You think he might be sick. You could contact the

_____.

5. You are putting in a rock garden. You would like a book that tells you all about the best kinds of flowers and plants to use. You could contact the _____.

6. You decide to add a porch to your house. You need someone to draw up the plans. You could contact the _____.

7. The porch costs more money than you thought. You don't have enough money and decide to get a loan. You could contact the

_____.

8. Your pipes are leaking. Your drains are clogged. Your faucets are dripping. You could contact the _____.

9. You decide to put an additional outlet in your kitchen to use for your new microwave oven. You could contact the _____.

10. Your doctor prescribed a medication. You think it is making you sick to your stomach. You need to know about the drug's side effects. You could contact the

_____.

Occupational Titles

Directions Match the occupational titles with the service each worker provides. Write the letter of the title before the correct service. You may use a dictionary.

Occupational Titles

A attorney	**H** chef	**O** veterinarian
B horticulturist	**I** podiatrist	**P** psychiatrist
C pharmacist	**J** editor	**Q** chiropractor
D dental hygienist	**K** barber	**R** nutritionist
E accountant	**L** architect	**S** dermatologist
F plumber	**M** contractor	**T** text processor
G real estate agent	**N** tailor	**U** auto mechanic

EXAMPLE ____U____ repairs cars

Services

1. _____ sews, repairs, or alters clothing

2. _____ treats nervous or mental disorders

3. _____ designs buildings

4. _____ prepares financial statements

5. _____ sells and rents homes

6. _____ installs and repairs pipes

7. _____ cleans teeth

8. _____ arranges to have work performed by hiring other people

9. _____ fills prescriptions written by medical doctors

10. _____ prepares food and creates recipes

11. _____ cuts and styles hair

12. _____ treats animals that are sick

13. _____ treats problems with feet

14. _____ treats people by manipulating the spinal column

15. _____ decides what to publish in a newspaper

16. _____ prepares documents using a word processor

17. _____ treats diseases of the skin

18. _____ plans diets and special menus; investigates the value of foods

19. _____ writes legal documents; represents people in a court of law

20. _____ grows flowers, shrubs, fruits, and vegetables

Organizations

Directions Match each word with its correct meaning. Write the letter
of your answer on the line provided. You may use a dictionary.

EXAMPLE ___A___ Union

A a group of workers who form an organization

Words

_____ **1.** consumer

_____ **2.** expert

_____ **3.** credentials

_____ **4.** profession

_____ **5.** trade

_____ **6.** apprentice

_____ **7.** foreman

_____ **8.** contractor

_____ **9.** intern

_____ **10.** journeyman

Meanings

A a person who has training and knowledge about a certain subject

B a job that requires a college education

C a boss or supervisor

D an occupation that requires a manual or mechanical skill

E a worker who is learning a trade

F proof that a person is an expert in a certain occupation

G a person who spends money on goods or services

H a person who agrees to perform work or provide supplies

I a worker who has completed an apprenticeship

J a professional worker who is practicing under the supervision of an experienced worker

Getting Help from Organizations

Directions Read each situation. Choose the organization from the list that you could contact for each situation. Write the name of the organization on the line provided.

> Medical Bureau or Medical Society
> Better Business Bureau
> Welcome Wagon or Welcome, Neighbor
> Chamber of Commerce
> Travelers Assistance or Travelers Aid
> Legal Aid Society

EXAMPLE You arrive in a strange city. You need a hotel room, but you do not know where to go.
You could contact the **Travelers Assistance or Travelers Aid** .

1. You want to start a business. You decide to form your own corporation. You need advice.

   You could contact the _____.

2. You just moved into Happy Villa. You don't know where any stores or doctors are. You need information about this new town.

   You could contact the _____.

3. You've been thinking about visiting Houston, Texas. You want the names of hotels, restaurants, and places to visit.

   You could contact the _____.

4. You want to roof your house. You've chosen a roofer. You want to know something about the roofer's service record.

   You could contact the _____.

5. You broke a bone. You are in a lot of pain. You are new in town and don't know a doctor.

   You could contact the _____.

Personal Information

Part A Complete this worksheet by providing important facts about yourself.

EXAMPLE Write your complete mailing address on the lines provided.

Ms. Patricia Shukert

1611 Pond Meadow Drive

Apt. 101

Fort Worth, TX 76109

Write your complete mailing address on the lines provided. Use the example as a guide.

1. _____

2. _____

_____

3. _____

4. Write your full name. _____

5. Write your signature. _____

6. Write your Social Security number. _____

7. Write your place of birth. _____

8. Write your date of birth. _____

9. Write your home telephone number. _____

10. Write your initials. _____

Part B Complete each sentence with the correct term.

EXAMPLE Use your full or _legal_ name when completing forms.

---

1. A person who was not born in the United States can become a _____ citizen.

2. A _____ card allows people who are not citizens to work in the United States.

3. You will need a Social Security number to file a _____ return.

4. To apply for a Social Security card, you must show your _____ certificate.

5. A paper that gives information to another person is a _____.

Job Application Forms

Directions Unscramble these words. Then use the words to complete the sentences below.

EXAMPLE	**Scrambled Word**	**Unscrambled Word**
	EWTNEVRII	INTERVIEW _____

Scrambled Words	**Unscrambled Words**
1. PPIINOTAACL	_____
2. BLIAVEALA	_____
3. TEPTNEIRN	_____
4. EPCALBIPAL	_____
5. YLMEPERO	_____
6. ACDUNITOE	_____
7. LPMYEOEE	_____
8. RESNWAS	_____
9. ITISNOPO	_____
10. UTGNSRIEA	_____

11. Before the job interview, Yolanda was asked to fill out a job _____.

12. A person who works for someone else is a(n) _____.

13. The name of your job is your _____.

14. Some forms may have questions that are not _____ to you.

15. You will have to supply information about your _____ when applying for a job.

16. You are considered _____ on the day you can start a job.

17. To show that all the information on your form is true, write your _____ at the end.

18. Before applying for a job, identify all the _____ skills you have.

19. Print the _____ to all questions as you complete a form.

20. The person who pays your salary is your _____.

Filling Out Job Application Forms

Part A Below is a list of terms that can be found on job applications. Before each term in column A, write the letter of its meaning found in column B.

| EXAMPLE | __A__ applicable | **A** something that is appropriate or suitable |

Terms

Meanings

_____ **1.** position

_____ **2.** full name

_____ **3.** education

_____ **4.** personal information

_____ **5.** employer

_____ **6.** pertinent

_____ **7.** experience

_____ **8.** major

_____ **9.** employee

_____ **10.** available

A the person or company that pays you a salary

B name of job you want

C when you can begin a job

D an area of study in which a student spends the most time and effort

E your whole legal name

F a person who works for someone else

G courses and programs from a school or college

H the same kind of work that you have done before

I facts about yourself

J related to the matter at hand

Part B There are two correct forms of printing for a job application. One correct form is all capital letters. The second correct form has capital letters only at the beginning of words and small letters everywhere else.

Directions Following are some samples of the way people filled in an application. If the printing is correct, write *C* on the line before the number. If the printing is incorrect, write *I* on the line before the number. Then print it correctly. The first one is done for you.

__I__ **1.** HAROLD p. dAVIS   Harold P. Davis *or* HAROLD P. DAVIS

_____ **2.** 3113 CLARK LANE

_____ **3.** February 14

_____ **4.** SuN ORder CompAny

_____ **5.** Cashier

_____ **6.** Ms. JAne Q. DAvis

_____ **7.** 210 Snowhill Court

_____ **8.** DRAKE HIGH SCHOOL

_____ **9.** BUSINESS EDUCATION

_____ **10.** RelAtionship: MOTHER

Job Application Acrostic

Directions Read each clue. Fill in the blanks with the word or words that match each clue. Then solve the acrostic message.

1. A form used to make a request

   — — — — — — — — — — —
   1   5   5   10   7   6   1   4   7   15   12

2. Printed document with spaces to fill in information

   — — — —
   3   15   9   13

3. A nine-digit identification number (2 words)

   — — — — — —   — — — — — — — —
   2   15   6   7   1   10   2   16   6   14   9   7   4   17

4. Person belonging to a country

   — — — — — — —
   6   7   4   7   11   16   12

5. Appropriate, suitable

   — — — — — — — — — —
   1   5   5   10   7   6   1   8   10   16

6. A paper with information

   — — — — — — — —
   18   15   6   14   13   16   12   4

7. Your name as you write it

   — — — — — — — — —
   2   7   19   12   1   4   14   9   16

8. Courses and programs from a school or college

   — — — — — — — — —
   16   18   14   6   1   4   7   15   12

9. The name of your job

   — — — — — — — —
   5   15   2   7   4   7   15   12

10. Boss or supervisor

   — — — — — — — —
   16   13   5   10   15   17   16   9

Acrostic Message

   — — — — — — — —   — — — — — —
   1   6   6   14   9   1   6   17   6   15   14   12   4   2

Previous Work Experience

Directions Complete this form using information from any previous work experience. Fill in all the spaces.

Employer _____

Address _____

Phone (_____) _____

Supervisor _____

Dates employed: from _____ / _____ / _____ to _____ / _____ / _____

Position title _____

No. hours worked/week _____

Salary: starting $_____ ☐ hourly ☐ weekly ☐ monthly

ending $_____ ☐ hourly ☐ weekly ☐ monthly

Description of work: _____

_____

_____

_____

Give name, address, and phone number of three references not related to you.

_____

_____

_____

_____

_____

_____

_____

Employment History

Employment History

List each job you have held. Start with your present or last job.
Include military service and volunteer activities.

1

Employer:	Dates		Work Performed
	From	To	
Address:			
Job Title:	Hrly. Rate/Salary		
Supervisor:	Starting	Final	
Reason for Leaving:			

2

Employer:	Dates		Work Performed
	From	To	
Address:			
Job Title:	Hrly. Rate/Salary		
Supervisor:	Starting	Final	
Reason for Leaving:			

Education	Elementary	High	College/University	Graduate/Professional
School Name				
Years Completed (Circle)	4 5 6 7 8	9 10 11 12	1 2 3 4	1 2 3 4
Diploma/Degree				
Describe Course of Study				
Describe Specialized Training, Apprenticeship, Skills, and Extracurricular Activities				

Honors Received:

State any additional information you think may be helpful to us in considering your application.

Agreement: The information given is correct. Any misrepresentation or omission found by the company at any time will be sufficient cause to terminate my employment. I authorize the company to obtain from others information pertinent to my employment.

Signature _____ Date _____

Financial Forms

Directions Match each meaning below with a term from the box.
Write your answers on the lines provided.

assets	deposit	liability	value
credit	finance charge	loan	withdrawal
debt	interest	net worth	

EXAMPLE __assets_____ property you own that has value.

1. _____ the value of your assets minus the value of your liabilities

2. _____ the amount of money your property is worth to a buyer

3. _____ a sum of money that you borrow

4. _____ the money you owe

5. _____ money owed, or liability

6. _____ a fee you pay on money you owe to a business

7. _____ the time you get to pay for the goods you buy

8. _____ money you put into an account

9. _____ money you take out of an account

10. _____ the money a bank pays you for putting money into a savings account

Establishing Credit

Directions Fill out this application for a charge account. You have been a teacher for five years. Use your school's address and phone number for place of employment. You are earning $1,200.00 biweekly (double this for your monthly salary or divide by two for your weekly salary). You are 30 years old, married, with two children. While in college, you worked as a cook for Frank's Carryout for three years earning $100.00 a week. You have a savings account with Chester Savings and Loan at 1010 Smith Street. You own a three-year-old Dodge Neon financed by your bank. Your driver's license number is 558-321-7766R. Your only credit reference is Money America, 710 East Avenue. Your account number is 00221, and there is no balance.

CREDIT APPLICATION for SMITH'S DEPARTMENT STORE

Last Name	First	Initial	Birthdate	Dependents	Social Security No.	☐ Own ☐ Rent

Present Address (Street & Number)	Payment or Rent $	How long were you at address?	Name and Address of Landlord or Mortgage Holder	

City State Zip	Home Telephone	Previous Address		How long were you at address?

Applicant's Employer	Business Address		How long were you at this job?

Position	Salary			Business Telephone
	Wk	Mo	Yr	

Previous Employer	Position		Salary	How long were you at this job?

Name and Address of Nearest Relative Not Living with You		Telephone

Other Source of Income (Income from alimony, child support or separate maintenance payments need not be disclosed if you do not wish to have it considered as a basis for repaying this obligation.) Annual Amount _____ How Long _____ Source _____

Bank	Branch	☐ Checking ☐ Savings ☐ Loan

Make of Car and Year	Financed by	Driver's License No.

CREDIT REFERENCES

Name	Address	Acct. No.	Balance

Reading Catalogs

Directions Read each catalog description. Then answer the questions.

> **The Pile-Lined Coat**
> A dressy look for winter. Outer material is 100% cotton, lined with alpaca-like acrylic pile for warmth. Four-button front, with handwarmer pockets, inner pocket, inner storm cuffs, quilted sleeve lining. Belted at the waist. Dry clean. Tan. Men's even sizes 40–44. Women's even sizes 8–14. Men's 7994536 Women's 7994535 **$130.00**

EXAMPLE   What order number would you use to get a men's coat? **7994536**

1. What are the two types of fabric used to make this coat? _____

2. Can you order this coat in a color other than tan? _____

3. Did the manufacturer use alpaca wool to make this coat? _____

4. Does this coat have a belt? _____

5. If you wear a women's size 6, can you order this coat in your size? _____

> **Winter Caps**
> This warm cap is 100% wool. Great for skating, running, skiing. Choose navy or red. One size fits all. 8765490 **$5.00** (Two for **$9.50**)

6. How much does one of these winter caps cost? _____

7. How much would you save if you bought two caps? _____

8. Could you order a cap in yellow? _____

9. In what sizes does the cap come? _____

10. What order number would you use to buy this cap? _____

Internet Shopping

Directions The following steps for shopping online are out of order. Put the steps in the correct order by numbering the spaces provided.

(EXAMPLE)   __2__ Search different Web sites for the product you want.

__1__ Turn on the computer.

_____ Give your payment information.

_____ Go to the checkout.

_____ Check the summary of your order.

_____ Turn on the computer.

_____ Search different Web sites for the product you want.

_____ Submit your completed order online.

_____ Look for an e-mail that confirms your online order.

_____ Look at different Web sites to compare prices.

_____ Select a product and put it in your shopping cart.

_____ Give your name and address.

Ordering Products

Part A Beside each term in Column A, write the letter of the correct meaning found in Column B.

EXAMPLE   __A__ item number   **A** number used to identify an item

Terms		Meanings
_____	**1.** quantity	**A** money you are charged for having items sent to you
_____	**2.** item price	**B** the price for one item
_____	**3.** total price	**C** number of items ordered
_____	**4.** shipping charges	**D** the total amount of money owed, including total price, tax, and shipping charges
_____	**5.** total charge	**E** the item price multiplied by the quantity

Part B Answer the questions below about this sample order form.

EXAMPLE   How many of each item was ordered? __2 sweatshirts; 1 pair of work boots__

Send to: Name _Robert D. Jones_
Address _345 Charter Avenue_
City/State/ZIP _Albuquerque, New Mexico 87106_

Item No.	Qty.	Size	Color	Description	Shipping Wt. lb.	oz.	Item Price	Total Price
756F	2	M	Red	Sweatshirt	1	8	$20.00	$40.00
8246	1 Pair	10	Black	Steel-Toe Work Boots	6	3	$61.99	$61.99

Shipping Charges by Weight	
Up to 10 lb. $3.00	
10 lb. to 20 lb. $4.00	
20 lb. to 30 lb. $5.00	
Over 30 lb. $6.00	

Total shipping weight   7   11

* Iowa residents add 6% sales tax.

Total Price	$101.99
*Sales Tax	.00
Shipping Charge	$3.00
Total Charge	$104.99

1. Who will receive this order? _____

2. Where will the order be sent? _____

3. What is the most expensive item ordered? _____

4. What is the total shipping weight? _____

5. What is the total amount owed by the customer? _____

Ordering from a Catalog

Directions Below are three items from a catalog page and an order form.
Order one of each item—A, B, and C. You want the items sent to your
home address. Fill in all necessary information on the order form. You
may choose any color, size, or style that is offered.

A WINNER II ATHLETIC SHOE — Uppers:
nylon and leather. Cushioned tricot lining.
Padded tongue and top-line. Imported heels.
Treaded rubber sole. Sponge rubber lining,
extra arch padding. State size needed—
Medium width only.

72G5641F Powder blue/navy
72G5643F Royal blue/white
72G5645F Black/silver
72G5647F Brown/tan

Shpg. wt. 1 lb., 7 oz. $44.99

B SWEATSHIRT WITH NOVELTY PRINT—
Acrylic and cotton fleece. Crew neck and raglan
sleeves. Specify style.

Sizes — S, M, L, XL
40G1721L   Baseball Shirt
40G1723L   Basketball Shirt
40G1725L   Football Shirt
40G1727L   Hockey Shirt

Shpg. wt. 6 oz. $9.99

C WOOL CREWNECK SWEATER: State size needed.

COLOR	MEN'S SIZES S, M, L	WOMEN'S SIZES S, M, L
RED	40H2015F	40H2217F
GREEN	40H2016F	40H2214F
BLUE	40H2014F	40H2218F
Shpg. wt.	5 oz.	5 oz.
Price	$49.99	$49.99

Send to: Name _____

            Address _____

            City/State/ZIP _____

Item No.	Qty.	Size	Color	Description	Shipping Wt. lb. oz.	Item Price	Total Price

Total shipping weight	**Total Price**
	*Sales Tax
	Shipping Charge
	Total Charge

Shipping Charges by Weight
Up to 10 lb. $3.00
10 lb. to 20 lb. $4.00
20 lb. to 30 lb. $5.00
Over 30 lb. $6.00

* Maine residents add 5% sales tax.

Filling Out an Order Form

Directions Below are sample items from a catalog page and the order form. Order at least three different items from the samples. You want the items sent to your home address. Fill in all necessary information on the order form.

CATALOG ENVELOPES (250 per box)
- Handles big jobs
- Save up to 40%
- Heavy gummed flaps

AD6-TR98	$9\frac{1}{2}$" x $12\frac{1}{2}$"	$25.79
AD6-TR99	10" x 13"	$27.29
AD6-TR100	$11\frac{1}{2}$" x $14\frac{1}{2}$"	$32.87

Shipping weight . . . . 12 lb.

WALL CHARTS
- Save 20%
- 1 free write-on/wipe-off pen with each chart

AD4-WC201   17" x 22" $21.98

Shipping weight . . . . 12 oz.

BUSINESS ENVELOPES (500 per box)
- Window style features frosted see-through panel
- Diagonal cut
- White weave   (4 or more boxes)

AD9-QS99	10" Plain	$10.05	$19.00
AD9-QS101	10" Window	$11.95	$20.70

Shipping weight . . . . 7 lb.

Send to: Name _____

Address _____

City/State/ZIP _____

Item No.	Qty.	Size	Color	Description	Shipping Wt. lb.	oz.	Item Price	Total Price

Total shipping weight			Total Price	
			*Sales Tax	
			Shipping Charge	
			Total Charge	

Shipping Charges by Weight
Up to 10 lb. $3.00
10 lb. to 20 lb. $4.00
20 lb. to 30 lb. $5.00
Over 30 lb. $6.00

* Colorado residents add 6% sales tax.

Returning Products

When returning products, your letter of complaint should be clear and polite. It should not be rude or threatening. Remember to include the following information in your letter.

- The date
- Your address
- The name of the company
- Your name

If you do not know the name of the person to write to, use *Dear Sir or Madam* as the greeting. Explain exactly what the problem is and what you would like the company to do about it.

Read this letter of complaint.
Notice the mistakes.

Dear Company:
   The CD you sent me was cracked. I am really mad. Send me a new CD right away or I will cause you some trouble. Hurry up.

       Yours truly,
       Tom

Directions Use the information in the box below to write a correct letter of complaint.

Majestic Flashlight Model #27
Price $5.65
The Wilmar Flashlight Company
3025 West Street
Buckingham, Iowa 52601

Tom Martin
1583 Milton Blvd.
Laurel, California 94939
August 12, (current year)

Addressing an Envelope

Two addresses belong on an envelope. The name and address of the person sending the letter go in the upper left-hand corner. The name and address of the person receiving the letter go in the middle of the envelope.

Directions Look at the names and addresses below. Place them correctly on the envelope. Put a comma between the name of the city and the state. Use the post office abbreviation for each state. Make sure to label the stamp with the correct amount for first-class postage.

The Sender:
Alice Barton
723 N. Quinn St.
Arlington Va. 22209

The Receiver:
Mrs. Edith Carlson
5489 Elk Rd.
Northfield Minn. 55057